CONTENTS

Karen grew up in a small town in north-eastern Victoria, Australia where she rode horses through a beautiful landscape of eucalypts, lakes, and snow-capped mountains. Her love of country continues to influence both her fiction and nonfiction writing. She built a career in a range of educational settings culminating in heading Australia's first writing and publishing degree. She holds a Ph.D. and M.Ed. (Hons) in the areas of myth and fantasy as well as a range of post-graduate qualifications in Education, ESL, and Literacy. Karen travels extensively overseas but enjoys nothing more than camping in the Australian Outback.

In the Company of Birds - Poems from an Outback Odyssey is Karen's second book to use poetry to explore the power of journeying. She is also the author of 17 fantasy novels. She lives in Melbourne and writes full time. You can find out more about Karen and her books on her website.

Connect with K.S. Nikakis

Amazon: https://www.amazon.com/author/ksnikakis
Twitter: https://twitter.com/KSNikakis
Facebook: www.facebook.com/ksnikakis
Goodreads: www.goodreads.com
Website: www.ksnikakis.com
Email: author@ksnikakis.com

WORKS BY K S NIKAKIS

Non Fiction
Travel and Poetry

Journey: Seeking the Sacred, Spirit and Soul
in the Australian Wilderness
In the Company of Birds: Poems from an
Outback Odyssey

Fantasy Novels
Series

Angel Caste series:
Angel Blood
Angel Breath
Angel Bone
Angel Bound
Angel Blessed
Angel Caste – Complete 5 Book Series

The Kira Chronicles trilogy:*
The Whisper of Leaves
The Song of the Silvercades
The Cry of the Marwing
remnant hard copies only

The Kira Chronicles series:
The Whisper of Leaves
The Silence of Stone

The Secrets of Stars
The Thunder of Hoofs
The Crying of Birds
The Music of Home
The Kira Chronicles – Complete 6 Book Series

Fantasy Novels

The Emerald Serpent
Heart Hunter
The Third Moon
Messenger
I Heard the Wolf Call My Name – *Finalist -*
Best YA Novel Aurealis Awards, 2019

Fantasy Novels – YA

The Dragon of the Drowned World

Fantasy Short Stories

The Gift
The Tale of Prince Anura
Dragon Sprite
Glass-Heart – *Finalist –*
Best YA Short Story Aurealis Awards, 2019
Ghost Stream
The White Stag
Rite

In the Company of Birds
Poems from an Outback Odyssey

K.S. NIKAKIS

First published by SOV CONSULTING LLC - SOV Media
Australia 2025
Amazon: www.amazon.com.au

In the Company of Birds - Poems from an Outback Odyssey
© copyright by KS Nikakis 2025

KS Nikakis asserts the right to be identified as the author of
In the Company of Birds - Poems from an Outback Odyssey.

Publisher: SOV CONSULTING LLC - SOV Media Melbourne,
Australia.

Cover: C Nikakis
Image: K.S. Nikakis
Typography: Adobe Brushscript; Benguiat Std.

National Library of Australia
Cataloguing-in-Publication entry: Nikakis, Karen Simpson

In the Company of Birds - Poems from an Outback Odyssey
ISBN 978-0-6451927-2-8

For my fellow seekers

Map of the Journey

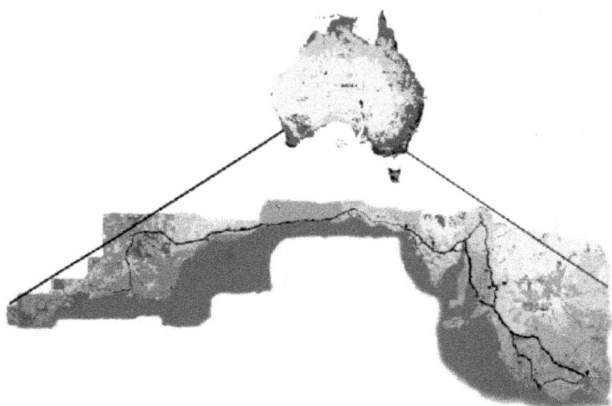

IN THE COMPANY OF BIRDS

POEMS FROM AN OUTBACK ODYSSEY

The birds are always with me, sometimes seen, sometimes only hinted at but always there. The blink of the sun as a raptor powers overhead, the fleeting shadow across the trail of something faster than my eye, the stir and still of bushes by flashing avian gems. I start to see them on this journey through Australia's southern wilderness because even in their absence, they're never truly gone. Shadows, distant songs, tracks in the dust, breeze-blown feathers at my feet. The birds that I felt a deep, inexpressible love for as a child but forgot in the frenetic demands of adulthood, return in all their splendour.

I open the door to a place of space and stillness and they are there.

In a journey of deliberate slowness, of intentional pauses to look and see and breathe, my long lost birds reappear. What is their story? What is mine? These questions might be too profound or too human to answer, and as my journey progresses, I wonder why I ask them at all. The birds are simply here, as I am, our lives separate but entwined, the weave of life and death, beauty and ugliness.

Even so, they demand I tell of them, and what better way than through poetry, the language of the spirit and soul. And so I write, each and every day, in the company of birds. But I'm getting ahead of myself in telling of my journey through Australia's southern wilderness.

If I were writing a travelogue, I would say I left Melbourne (with my husband and our caravan) on Friday June 23, 2023, and on Friday August 11, 2023, 50 days and over 6,918 kms (4,298 mls) later, I returned. In that time I explored the Nullarbor's vast sweep, the Great Western Woodland (larger than England and Wales combined), the Bight's soaring cliffs, Cape Le Grand's pristine silica beaches, and the towering Karri forests of the south west, all in the company of birds. But this is not primarily a travelogue, it is a story about birds and what they gifted me, and so let me make a beginning.

The Journey Begins

Introduction

Ragged Blue

Being from Melbourne, Victoria, means that to head west, we must first head north (or take a dip in the Southern Ocean). Our first stop is Kaniva, a small town of 891 (according to the latest Census). We choose Kaniva as we've stayed at its great little caravan park before and as the van's stored off site, we need to fill our water tanks. Most of our journey will be through desert country and there's often no drinking water even in caravan parks and no water at all at Free Camps where we'll mainly stay.

It's a day of low grey cloud and spits of rain as we leave the city behind, which is fairly typical of Melbourne's winter where June temperatures range from 8 to 15C (46-59F). The days can be gloomy but they're rarely really cold.

The passing paddocks are green and the dams full and when we break at Lake Burrumbeet, the silvery light creates bright reflections on the water's clear surface. The lake's clarity is ironic given its name supposedly comes from the First Nation word *burrmbidj* which means muddy or dirty water.

We pass through Ararat and Horsham, and then the Grampians rise in a ragged blue silhouette along the horizon, always striking despite their familiarity from our many visits.

The land flattens and dries as we near the Little Desert National Park. We're in wheat country now and silos rise from the land like ancient monuments. I watch for birds but it's the sky that captures my attention.

The Sky's a Galah

The sky's a galah
clouds all pinks and greys
but then the wind parts
its soft feathers
to reveal the skin beneath
as white
as the haft of
an arrow

Kaniva to Peterborough
Day 2 Saturday June 24

The Birds Know

I only ever feel I've begun a journey in Australia when I've crossed the Victorian border. Tasmania might be Australia's smallest state but Victoria's familiarity makes it feel small, and it *is* small (227,600 sq kms/87,876 sq mls) compared to South Australia (983,482 sq kms/ 379,724 sq mls) and the giant of Western Australia (at 2,527,013 sq kms/975,685 sq mls). But it's not just size that tells me home is now behind me; it's the broader, browner landscape.

Crossing the Victorian – South Australian border is a simpler process now the border closures of the Covid Pandemic have eased, but not one without restrictions. The interstate transfer of most fresh fruit and vegetables is prohibited to avoid the spread of certain pests and diseases, and while there are warning signs and disposal bins, the actual Quarantine Station is on South Australia's far side. Given we've cooked or eaten our fresh produce, we have no need to stop.

We break at Murray Bridge for a pub lunch overlooking the broad sweep of the Murray River. The town was renamed in 1924 in honour of the new road and rail bridge, but were we to trek backwards in time, we would be lunching at Edwards Crossing, and before that at Mobilong, and originally at Pomberuk.

The Murray River makes up most of Victoria's northern border. Rising in the Snowy Mountains (on Australia's east coast), it winds west for 2,530 kms (1,572 mls) bordered by irrigated farm lands, unique river redgum forests, and extensive wetlands, before it exits into the sea near Goolwa, South Australia.

From my vantage point in the pub, I can see water birds circling above the Murray and pelicans drifting on its calm waters but hear no bird song thanks to the pub's closed windows.

We continue to our second night's destination of Peterborough, a small town with a steam train heritage we've explored on earlier visits. We pull into the small park we've stayed at before and, as the light fades, I grab my phone camera and set out in search of birds. The dusk is full of the sweet and complex songs of magpies but also the harsher, simpler songs of ravens, and I let them wash over me, familiar but strangely unfamiliar, thanks to my new surroundings.

Time to Leave

The birds know when it's time
to leave
the clouds clear
and the air heaves with damp
then the trees empty
and the sky fills with
the quiet that sings
of frost

Peterborough to Mt Little Station
Day 3 Sunday June 25

Curved-beak Birds

We head northwards the next morning through Orroroo to Hawker and deep into the Flinders Ranges. There's something magical about the Flinders Ranges, perhaps because they were my first introduction to the Outback over forty years ago. The whole area is ruggedly beautiful and historically rich (both in First Nation and European terms) and we've visited it many times and explored it in depth in 2021.

The Ranges' rugged outlines, formed by sediment laid down by ancient seas and later tipped on its side by the earth's upheavals, are the glorious rust-reds and sage-greens typical of the Australian Outback.

We join our friends camping at Mt Little Station, a working sheep and cattle station (ranch) that offers tourist accommodation. Many stations run camping grounds to off set the effects of droughts, floods, and global trade on their business. Some even offer showers and toilets in addition to the wonderful scenery normally locked away from public view. Mt Little has a bit of each: toilets that require a hike, showers that need a drive, and a rugged sweep of spectacular mountains.

Butter the Sky

We are in the Flinders Ranges
with its dried-blood sands
and mobs of lime-green budgies
that rise in flocks
to butter the sky

there are curve-beaked birds too
bigger and less pretty
that wait on the verges
for the roadkill
we might deliver

Mt Little Station
Day 4 Monday June 26

Sky-borne Ships

Pelicans

Pelicans fly in strict formation
like sky-borne ships
solemn, disciplined

demanding respect
despite the flap
of their slack
pink jowls

Mt Little Station to Wudinna Free Camp
Day 5 Tuesday June 27

Feathers Too Soft

We swap campsites for our final night at the station as rain is forecast and there are floodable creeks between us and the highway. As it turns out, the great slab of rainfall (one of many that soaks much of Australia on this journey) stays north and we stay dry. We head off with the group and stop at Hawker, another great little Outback town, to fill our water tanks and empty our toilet (the two musts of any camping trip).

We intended to visit Lake Gairdner which, when in flood, is the third biggest salt lake in Australia, but it's water that stops us. Most Outback roads are unsealed and can be corrugated and dusty in summer or worse (depending on when the bulldozer went through) and impassable after rain in winter, and the very wet road into Lake Gairdner is now closed.

We follow the Flinders Ranges Way south through Quorn to Port Augusta (because there's only a tangle of tracks west) and then delay at Port Augusta in an attempt (unsuccessful, we later discover) to have our hot water system repaired. We spend a lot of time and money on caravan maintenance but as a fellow camper once ruefully remarked to us: *There's always something to be done on a caravan.*

Port Augusta (population 14,102) sits at the head of the spectacular Spencer Gulf and the drive over the Joy Baluch Bridge which spans it (named after a former mayor of Port Augusta who served for 29 years) is utterly breath-taking.

Silver gulls hang in the stiff breeze brilliant against the great sweeps of water north and south.

We continue on through Kimba, home to the eye-catching Big Galah, eight metres tall and resplendent in its new coat of paint. Kimba's claim to fame, apart from the Big Galah, is its position at the halfway point across Australia, as measured between Perth and Sydney as the crow (or in this case, galah) flies. Kimba is also super welcoming of campers and we've stayed at its small Free Camp before. We don't stop this time because we're playing catch up with our friends who have reached our next camp at Wudinna.

The word *wudinna* is thought to mean *granite hill* in the language of the local First Nations people (although such namings can be disputed). Regardless of the accuracy of its name, Wudinna's *granite hill* is one of the largest granite monoliths in the Southern Hemisphere.

We pass through the town (population 1,164) to join our friends amongst the granite's undulations, their curves reminiscent of the wonderful Kata Tjuta (in the Uluru-Kata Tjuta National Park, Northern Territory). These stones are grey-green, not red like Kata Tjuta, thanks to their coat of lichen, and are smaller, cradling sublimely beautiful lakes on their summits that shine despite the deepening dusk.

Today We Killed a Bird

Today we killed a bird
which flew
bright as flame
under the car
its feathers too soft
to leave a mark

Wudinna Free Camp
Day 6 Wednesday June 28

Birds Are No Preachers

Mob Birds

Corellas are mob birds
hanging with friends and enemies
and mere acquaintances

yelling like football crowds
that support opposing teams
shouting each other down

tirelessly

endlessly

Preachers

Last night apostlebirds flew
to where we camped
the rock called
Weedna or Wudinna

the name's changed
over time
but apostlebirds have kept theirs
despite their number being
larger or smaller than
their Christian namesakes

these birds are no preachers
content to let the stone speak
for itself in all
its multitude of languages

Wudinna Free Camp to Minnipa Free Camp
Day 6 Wednesday June 28

Birds Swoop Low

Minnipa is just 37 kms (23 mls) further west and another small town (population 168) with fabulous rock formations, in this case, the massive granite dome of Tcharkuldu Rock, the striking black streaked 'waves' of Pildappa Rock (a pink inselberg or isolated rock hill – Uluru being a bigger and more famous version), and the smaller granite dome of Polda Rock. We Free Camp at Tcharkuldu Rock right at the rock's feet and walk/drive to explore the other nearby formations.

While the more famous Wave Rock in Western Australia is slightly longer and a lot higher (110 metres long v.100 metres, and 8 metres tall v. 3-4 metres) Pildappa has the same awe-inspiring sense as the iconic Valley of the Winds walk at Kata Tjuta. The stone rises as gently as a rust-red ocean swell, striped and stained, and in some places dips to hold quiet pools of shadow. More people explore its clefted head than walk its feet and I am happy to be alone with the early wattle, shining slides of water, and distant symphony of birds.

Minnipa Free Camp
Day 7 Thursday June 29

Ducks Are a Pair

Watery Corpses

Birds swoop low over still water
to join their reflections
briefly, beautifully

then separate to rise
bellies full of watery
corpses

leaving the pool
grave-marked
with ripples

Two Ducks

The ducks are a pair of
synchronised swimmers
with twin wakes

they bob in unison
then launch
with matched
wingbeats

to leave
dual furrows

Minnipa Free Camp to Streaky Bay
Day 7 Thursday June 29

Shapes of Birds

The Eyre Highway drapes like necklace around the top of the Eyre Peninsula, dipping south after Kimba and rising north again as it passes through Wudinna and Minnipa and on towards Ceduna. We turn west well before then, at Poochera, taking the Streaky Bay Road south west to the coast.

Our friendship group has dwindled to two couples and we are to camp at Streaky Bay, a popular holiday destination in summer when its population of 2,081 multiplies many times. We were last here in 2021 and then, as now, its pier is crowded with cormorants and pelicans that are completely undisturbed by the stream of photo-happy tourists.

Campers with all sorts of rigs stop to fuel up, eat, and enjoy the birds as we do but our destination's ten minutes further on and we soon head off. The park's right on the beach and over the following days, we're treated to magnificent sunrises, sunsets, and a multitude of birds.

The Sign

The sign is made of rusted steel
the shapes of birds
punched out
to leave their imprint
on the sky

eagle, emu, galah
magpie, cockatoo

aloft on wings of air
they come to earth in
in flakes of slow rust
like a drift of
orange feathers

The Song of Birds Unseen

Cloud brings a dull dawn
the pale sun to the east
soon swallowed
by the grey

but all around
the trees are alive
with the songs of
birds unseen

Streaky Bay
Day 8 Friday June 30 to Day 12 Tuesday July 4

Four Gulls Glide

Cormorant Island

There's an island close enough to see
the cormorants that crowd its stone
the way they stretch their wings
like ragged scarecrows
as if to ward off waves

the way they turn their heads
to admire the view
or their neighbours' profiles

the way they rise at dusk
haphazard and hungry
to make their way out
into the world

Sparrows Dine

Sparrows dine as we do
on pies and pasties and vanilla slices

they give the coffee a miss
though not by choice

their meal drops from ours
in beak-sized pieces
but the coffee remains
unspilled

Gulls I

The gulls are in full voice
but not, I guess
to exchange pleasantries

Hey there, Crook-beak, you stink of stale chips
Mind you're business, Muck-feather

yet not even frenemies
such as these
dispute each other's grace
as they skate on silver wings
above the salty crests
of waves

Gulls II

And out of a quiet dawn
of soft grey cloud
slit with gold
four gulls glide
at peace
like the
sea

Gulls III

Google lens tells me it's a Pacific Gull
that stands feathered shoulders above the silvers
to either side

brown-browed and beaked
indifferent to the pelicans' glide
its attention, like that of lesser birds
on the fishermen's reeking slops

as it waits to see
what might come

Dove

I pause at a grave
unsure whether it's an angel
or bird that adorns
the stone

a dove, I decide
suspended from a single
chunky wing
a spray of olive leaves
gripped tightly in its
beak

a sign from God to Noah
the Flood is over and
the Grace of God
restored

but there's no Grace here
for Martha
who died at 21 and
her infant son
who died
just seven months
later

Starlings

They're at it again
performing their high-wire act
with perfect poise

starlings

all in a line
on a line

like treble clefs
without the
harmony of
music

Nest

The sea has eaten
the stone away
and with each huge gulp
has deepened a ledge

that's filled with twigs
sea-silvered
not windblown
but collected

a bed for osprey hatchlings
to keep them safer
than the stone

Streaky Bay to Port Augusta
Day 13 Wednesday July 5

Red-daubed Throat

We farewell the other couple and reluctantly head east again, *reluctantly* because no traveller wants to U-turn and retrace their steps on any journey. Our hot water service still isn't working which means it must be replaced and that means we must return to Port Augusta.

The land looks different from an easterly direction and fascinating despite my frustration. We stop at Kimba to fuel up and I take a closer look at their freshly painted Big Galah, one of many 'big things' in Australia (like bananas, rams, crayfish, and pineapples).

The galah's a brighter pink with motifs that at first glance look like First Nation symbols but on closer inspection turn out to be flowers. The design on its grey wings is different again, reminiscent of the Haida art I fell in love with in Canada.

We move on to a nearby picnic spot for coffee and cake and the birds descend.

Wattlebird

A red wattlebird understands
the power of picnic tables
to draw the owners of food

and of the necessity of waiting
and of having manners

it flits from tree to tree
showing off its yellow breast
and red-daubed throat
to earn our admiration
and succeeds

to gain
its just reward

Silver Gulls

A wind sweeps over Spencer Gulf
in mighty gusts
the gulls astride its shoulders
more graceful than
my struggles on the earth below

the wind continues through the night
to bring a storm
that hurls the rain like gravel
and gift a dawn
washed clean

the bird song is purer
like church bells that ring
to celebrate the saving
of a soul

Port Augusta to Kimba Free Camp
Day 14 Thursday July 6

Silhouette the Trees

It's mid afternoon before the hot water system is installed and we're on our way west again. It's no hardship to repeat our crossing of the Spencer Gulf's vast sprawl of glittering water and the route is familiar too, given the number of times we've driven it recently. I video the highway's sweep, the fields of white-winged turbines, the sprawl of smoke-blue mountains and, as the land opens up, I sense something open up in me as well.

We stop at Kimba again, this time for the night at the Recreation Reserve, Kimba's second Free Camp. The Reserve has terrific facilities (donation encouraged and we comply, despite being self-contained) and is popular. Vans cluster near the ablution block but we set up on the other side with only trees for company.

Bird Dusk

Dusk descends
in a curtain of icy blue
and stars appear
tight pricks of light
folded in upon themselves
to escape the cold

the birds fare no better
their silhouettes in trees
soon eaten by the dark

Kimba Free Camp to Penong
Day 15 Friday July 7

Windmills

Our next stop is Penong and we keep a careful eye on the weather radar to track the great slabs of unseasonal rainfall that sweep across Australia. The rain keeps further north and is a key reason we chose to make this trip all about Australia's southern wilderness. We later meet a couple who did go north and spent five weeks in rain which is enough to (literally) dampen the spirits of even the most optimistic camper.

We've mostly enjoyed clear bright days and the bursts of rainfall have been brief and a boon to taking atmospheric pictures. The good weather continues as we pass through Wudinna and Minnipa again to Ceduna where we stayed in 2021 (having managed to cross into South Australia when the border briefly opened during the Covid lockdowns). On that journey, we used Ceduna as a base to explore the area's fabulous national parks and beaches, which is why we're not stopping on this journey.

We've passed through Penong many times without stopping too, despite its enticement as home to Australia's biggest windmill (with a span of over 10.6 metres/35 ft) but this time we're intent on a slower, more explorative trip, and book into Penong's lovely little park for two nights.

I explore the Windmill Museum, a collection of free standing windmills whose silver blades flash in the sun's last rays and, as dusk falls, reconnoitre the town's stone and corrugated iron out-buildings, remnants of a tougher pioneering past.

The next day, the clear skies give way to rain squalls and we have Cactus Beach (home to a famous surf break) all to ourselves. We see only a few people at the windswept Porte Le Hunte jetty and the spectacular Lake Macdonnell, with its pink waters striking against a back drop of creamy dunes and blue-black clouds, is also deserted, allowing us some spectacular shots.

Penong
Day 16 Saturday July 8

A Heron Rises

Murmuration

The sky's a fashionable
egg-shell blue
horizoned with a
dusty-rose
that fades to
stars

cold white beacons

that warn the birds
that night is coming

the birds take heed and murmurate
like swarming bees
and then disperse

as if they have
a hive to shelter in
as well

Glass Bird

An eagle hovers
above the Penong Hotel door
its static stained-glass wings
in perfect symmetry
as we pass
beneath

Idol

A goshawk perches on the cliff
god-like
framed by a crevice
like an idol in
a niche

it oversees the ocean
doused by sun and squalls
in equal measure

and then a heron
rises from the sands
on angel wings
grey as the sky

Penong to Whitewell Tank Free Camp
Day 17 Sunday July 9

Break Cover

In *Journey: Seeking the Sacred, Spirit and Soul in the Australian Wilderness (2020)*, I describe how, after a long day's drive and having passed closed Free Camps or missed them, Whitewell Tank Free Camp became our stop of last resort (the alternative being to sleep on the side of the road). But this trip, we know exactly where it is.

We arrive in daylight, the second van in, and have our choice of sites. The large sealed and fenced Free Camp sits just outside the gates to the Head of Bight Whale Watching Centre and many campers use the camp in readiness for the gates' opening the next morning. The flat surrounds provide sweeping vistas of sunrise and sunset and, as night falls, I watch the headlight beams dance like fireflies along the Eyre Highway to the north.

Grieve for Life

The land pulls the horizon sideways
to stretch the trees
and make them small and
many-stemmed

the parrots
emerald-daubed
dash across in front
the first we miss by a feather
the second by
my sharp inhalation
of breath

I know that parrots mate for life
and if one is lost the other
must surely grieve
for life

a burden
I have no wish
to bear

Wagtail

There are willie wagtails
that seem content to dance alone
but the sexes look the same
so maybe it's a Wendy not a Willie
that I watch
content with her lot in life
or sick of seeking mates
or simply on
a girl's day out
only she or he
can tell but
I do not speak
the language of their dance

Star Song

The birds do not compete
with the stars tonight
their songs are silent
unlike the sky
that roars its music

in torrents of layered silver
like a storming river
in flood

the music of the spheres seems fanciful
in daylight hours
but not when the stars press down
with the force
of an orchestra's
crescendo

Whitewell Tank Free Camp to Great Australian Bight Free Camp
Day 18 Monday July 10

Only Avians

The starry night gives way to a clear, blue-sky day, which makes me extra happy given it's my birthday and I plan to spend it staring out over the Southern Ocean from the cliffs of the Great Australian Bight. The cliffs range from 60-120 metres (200-400 ft) in height and I'm hoping the day stays still. Seeing passing whales would be the cherry on the top of the metaphorical cake but they're not necessary to my enjoyment.

There are many Free Camps along the cliffs, the tracks in signed and unsigned, and both types often hard to see. We search for a track I read of on social media, special because the indented cliffs allow views east and west as well as south. The track is supposed to be 52 kms east of the Western Australian border and we count the kilometres down but it's unmarked and hidden by bushes. We overshoot and have to U-turn, no mean feat given the combined length of the 4x4 and van. Tyre tracks tell us we're not the only ones to have missed the entrance which is steep, slanted, and stony but we end up exactly where we want to be.

There's another van there and we settle in for a day of shared campfire, shared wine, and shared joy in the ocean's magnificent blue. The air is mild and it seems hard to believe that were we to fly south like a sea bird, we would end up in Antarctica's icy wilderness.

Unwinged

On Australia's southern edge
the land falls into the sea
not gradually but
in one fell swoop
as if slashed

by a knife

not cleanly
but hacked away in chunks
by seas unwinged
by birds

no sea eagles or ospreys or even gulls
patrol the skies
the only avians
swallows and wagtails
whose dive and dance
seek to convince us
of their salty
credentials

Great Australian Bight Free Camp to Moodini Bluff Free Camp
Day 19 Tuesday July 11

A Raven Hops

It's a calm night for which we're grateful, given our camping companions' tale of all but being blown off the cliffs on a previous visit. The blue sky competes with the ocean's blue the next morning as we follow the stony track back to the Eyre Highway and head towards the Western Australian border. The Southern Ocean pounds the cliffs to our right while the Nullarbor National Park sprawls to our left. Along with the Regional Reserve, it holds the largest semi-arid karst (cave) landscape in the world. The caves, caused by collapses of the stone above, aren't visible from the highway and with the van on the back, we're unable to explore.

We pull up at the Quarantine Station as we must and the 4x4 and van are thoroughly checked. I've downloaded lists of things prohibited in each state and territory but the lists are never definitive and we hand over the fresh turmeric, (much to my husband's chagrin) only to have it returned after the Quarantine Officer consults a second list.

The land grows gradually hillier and the trees taller until we pull into our next Free Camp (Moodini Bluff) 219 kms (136 mls) west of the border. Free Camps (sometimes called Rest Areas) provide flat camping areas off the main roads, with the bigger ones having tracks and camping enclaves that extend for hundreds of metres into the trees. Most have rubbish bins, a few have picnic tables, and a very small number have pit toilets and dump points. Stone fireplaces are common but you need your own firewood. Popular Free

Camps are soon stripped of wood and wood collection is prohibited in National Parks as it removes animal habitat.

Campers usually arrive at Free Camps any time after noon and most will try to get some distance from the road because of roadtrain noise (which can sound as loud as actual trains). Roadtrains, along with kangaroos, are the reasons campers tend to avoid traveling at night. For those unfamiliar, roadtrains are trucks with up to four trailers attached which can measure over 50 metres in length. They are a major means of distributing goods in the Outback and go fast, can't swerve, and need lots of room to stop. (We've seen decapitated cattle on other trips we've guessed have stuck their head out onto the road.)

While kangaroos are smaller, they tend to be active at night, and can bound from bushes onto the road, or just sit on the road, dazzled by headlights. Hitting a kangaroo can prove fatal for both of you or cause a lot of damage, not just to the animal, but to your vehicle and van. The might of roadtrains, along with their bull bars, is why there are so many dead kangaroos on some roads.

The Free Camp already holds a scatter of vans and smoking campfires and I chat to my fellow campers as I wander about in the evening's golden light in search of birds.

Road Kill

A raven hops clear
just in time
reluctant to quit
the crimson smear
tyre-tracked
into the road

the meal seems better suited
to things with tongues
but the raven loiters
as if it knows that death
delivers life as well

Bell-pitched

We come in early
having gained time at the WA border
where the clocks turn back

it's a Free Camp with that magic thing
called Internet reception
which turns out to be the magic
of an immature witch
or mage
who lacks commitment

unlike the fanboy flies
who hover close

but there's music too
bell-pitched
of birds small and unmajestic
who sing the songs
of gods

Moodini Bluff Free Camp to Harm's Lake Free Camp
Day 20 Wednesday July 12

Bird Armies

Most Free Campers are out early, as we are, though not because we're in a rush. Early to bed means early to rise and it's another bright clear day as we rejoin the Eyre Highway, which is easy to do, given the scarcity of traffic. It's not long before the highway dips steeply to the Roe Plain in a sudden and surprising descent that always catches me unawares after hundreds of kilometres of flat sprawl. We pull into the roadhouse at Madura Pass for fuel where I chat to the young Scottish manager on a working holiday.

Roadhouses, the Outback's main source of fuel, groceries, and other basic supplies, used to be run by locals with a deep connection to and knowledge of the area's history and road conditions. It's a tough, isolated life and, as people aged, more were replaced by young tourists/backpackers on working holidays or working in the Outback as part of visa requirements. Covid border closures locked many out but they're back now and it's great to exchange experiences with people from places we've recently visited.

We are surrounded by trees as we drive on and there's no shortage of scenic sights. At 16,000,000 hectares (40,000,000 acres), the Great Western Woodland is larger than England and Wales combined and home to nearly 3,500 flowering plants and 215 species of birds. On previous trips I've been surprised by seeing so many trees on the Nullarbor Plain (*null arbor* means no trees) and this time is no exception.

The trees' openness (less than 30% canopy cover) tells me they're the 'woodland' part of the Woodlands, which includes vegetation types classified as mallee, grasslands, and sandplain shrublands. The gums shine in the dappled sunlight and bright yellow slashes tell of early wattles. I see or hear the usual galahs, parrots, ravens, and magpies rather than birds like the bush stone-curlew, bustard, or Carnaby's black cockatoo listed as making their home here. We don't stop to explore so it's likely they are deeper in the trees.

The clear day slowly fades to the glorious dusk only the Outback delivers. Shadows stripe the red earth and the westering sun gilds the gums an egg-yolk yellow. Then the horizon turns to ripe apricot and when the night sky follows, it delivers layer upon layer of stars.

We set a fire and watch the coals pulse gold and crimson and every shade of vermillion in between. Fire-watching might be an ancient pastime but it's lost none of its ability to calm, and centre, and reconnect the watcher with the things that matter most.

Beggars

The bird armies gather
when we stop to eat along the way
encouraged by my husband's
toss of crusts

yellow-throated miners threaten theft
and magpies mob

the juveniles
reckless
greedy
unlike the ravens

who keep their distance
disdainful so it seems
of the rabble hoi polloi

Harm's Lake Free Camp to Salmon Gums
Day 21 Thursday July 13

Bereft of Birds

All roads lead to Norseman in this part of the Outback but we stop there only to refill a gas bottle, fuel up with diesel, and restock the pantry before we turn south onto the Coolgardie-Esperance Highway. We're heading to Salmon Gums, a small town (population 196) named after the beautiful salmon-coloured barks of the local trees (eucalyptus salmonophloia). Salmon gums line the highway and beyond them we glimpse spectacular salt lakes, those with water filled with impossibly bright reflections.

There's nothing to be bought in Salmon Gums, including diesel and food, so we're pleased with our Norseman stop, but the small caravan park is a delight. It's neat and tidy with super friendly managers who set a communal fire each night. The quiet is punctured by enormously long ore trains that run close to the park. It's hard to count the trucks, given they are identical, but they take an age to pass.

Clad in Black

The biggest open woodland in the world
seems curiously bereft of birds
or perhaps it's just our engine noise
or heavy hum of tyres
or lack of pause
that keeps the landscape empty

we see in blurs
but the raven is clear
as it loiters nearby in search of roadkill
clad in its shine of undertaker black

Salmon Gums
Day 22 Friday July 14 to Day 23 Saturday July 15

Bird Song

After the Rains

After the rains
the sunlight colours
the young eucalypts
gold
and washes the bird song
silver
to chime like bells
within the trees

In Harmony with Birds

I've read that birds layer their songs
choosing a frequency unused
by others
and I imagine the sky
a vast harmonic cake
of many layers
each song distinct yet in accord
some as rich as chocolate
others some light confection
and I imagine that
we live in layers too
tilted perhaps by life's pressures
upended
like anticlines and synclines
our former and future lives packed tight
life before life and after death
in endless layering
like the songs
of birds

Shining

The day is a shining of
pink salmon gum trunks
garlanded in celebrations of bark
stripped away and
falling
amongst shadow and sun
in chaos patterns
that hide the sacred
in full view
the bird song light as bells
the only hint of glory

Salmon Gums to Cape Le Grand National Park
Day 24 Sunday July 16

The Raven Behind Me

It's another blue-sky day as the Coolgardie-Esperance Highway continues our journey south, back to the coast at Esperance. The sun gilds the salmon gums we pass and lights the still waters of the salt lakes with reflections more perfect than the things that they reflect.

We last visited Esperance over thirty years ago when it was filled with hot winds, smoke, and ash and as the bushfires crept closer, we packed up the tent and our two small children in the early hours and drove away.

There are no bush fires this time. The sky clouds over and when we reach Esperance, we dodge raindrops to search for a place to eat. I remember nothing about the town from our earlier visit, but it looks picturesque and the food is good, and having eaten, we head east and hug the coast to Cape Le Grand National Park.

The park is 32,000 hectares (79,703 acres) in size with beaches claimed to be amongst the most beautiful in the world. Their pristine white silica sand and clear aqua waters are certainly striking and we set up camp at Lucky Bay less than 50 metres from the water. The National Park campground is thoughtfully designed with environmentally friendly facilities but no power, drinking water, or dump point so you need to be self-contained.

The big sites are bordered with native bushes, some in flower, others like the banksia, mostly spent but with food enough for honey-eaters, and for the cockatoos and galahs keener on the rough cones of banksia seed.

Cape Le Grand National Park
Day 25 Monday July 17 to Day 26 Tuesday July 18

Eyes of Black

Sunrise I

I reach the beach before sunrise
the east as ripe as tangerines
the sands' cool silver
wave-imprinted

and then the sun breaks
on the bay's other side
and the raven behind me
launches
in celebration of the new day

its coal-black feathers
refuse the light
wanting to rejoice
in their own
endless night

Sunrise II

The bright pinks of sunrise
have blazed their orange and golds
and the seagull shapes that dive
to rise again
do not to settle
until the clouds have finished
their storms of colour
to arrive at last
at the whites and silvers
of the gulls' cool
plumage

Ravens and Crows I

I find it hard to tell crows from ravens
their songs seem similar
but the raven's more prone
to a trio of
descending notes

and in the end, I decide it's ravens
I hear singing
in the sparse-gummed woodlands
by the rust-red sage-green plains
on aqua shores of oceans
where the wind whips waves
to white horses with
foaming manes
and endless, endless tails

Honey-eater

It takes a while to snap the bird
that silhouettes amongst the trees
then flashes yellow tempting me
to name it

it lands on the path in front
as a couple stroll into view
and fail to pause

the bird is gone
but captured on my phone

a white-cheeked honey-eater or
a New Holland honey-eater
the first with eyes of black
the second with the white that gleams
back at me on this sunny day

the name's decided
not that the bird cares
it knows what it is
and seems at peace
with its place in
the world

Cape Le Grand National Park to Esperance
Day 27 Wednesday July 19

How Birds Sit in Water

We head west back to Esperance, the day as grey and rainy as the day we arrived there, as if all the blue skies and aqua seas of Cape Le Grand in between didn't happen. It's only 40 minutes to the caravan park near Pink Lake, the same one we stayed at all those years ago. Locals tell us the lake's no longer pink (thanks to an historical decision to change the water flows) but it doesn't matter. The glories of the local wetlands more than make up for the lake's lack of pink.

There are pools reminiscent of Florida's Everglades, with trees clad in ragged curtains of pale lichen, that stand knee-deep in black water soon spangled with rain drops. There's fluting bird calls and everything's a flash with light or gleaming in colours glossed by rain.

Black Cockatoos

Black cockatoos rise slowly
from the verge
too slowly I fear
for our speed of travel

their tail bands tell me
they're yellow-tailed black cockatoos
but Google says they're too far west
my next best guess is
Carnaby's black cockatoos
but they're too far east

they've got the same gung-ho attitude of every cockie
I've ever met
so maybe they've decided to perch within the liminal
just to tease each traveller with
their cheeky cockie test

Esperance
Day 28 Thursday July 20 to Day 30 Saturday July 22

A Heron Rises

Hidden

There are aqua bays
with white sand
and signs that warn of nesting plovers

the banksias are spent
bristle-cones with open mouths
the few pale
flower-heads full
of honey-eaters

pelicans glide
from one hidden lake to another

to tell me
there's a lot more here
than I can see

Birds at Rest

There are birds at rest on banks
of seaweed firm enough
to drive on
as vehicles do

but I walk
the fine silica sand
squeaking
under soles

birds skate the sky
scoop things from water
bob on waves

swap places with flock mates
in an endless shuffle between
sea and shore

Bird Hide

From the bird hide I see
dark shapes far off on
the lake's choppy surface

the sign tells me
how certain birds sit in water
the shape of beaks and bills
the way their tails perk up
or lay flat

and I compare them to
my phone's blurred images
without success

Cemetery I

The graves in the Pioneer section
are doused with shadows
thrown by trees that grow
thick and tall and strong

the names of those who lived
and died two centuries past
illegible or missing
the plots unmarked

a heron rises
the grey of ghosts
its brief flight
soon eaten by the trees

Cemetery II

After rain
the graves seem sharper
in their neat lines

they face the east
which means, for some
they face a fence

the birds face whatever
way they choose
and send their songs
across the empty sweep of land

a resting place for all the dead
to come

Cemetery III

I trace the song
full-voiced, melodious
to a pied currawong
perched atop a pencil pine
a cypress by another name
and common in these sites
of death

the crown bends
under its weight
dips then stills as the bird departs
taking with it all signs
of life

Sea Pigeons

The jetty's barred with smart bronze gates
that stop me in my tracks
but not the pigeons
who sun themselves on its seaward side
then rise in flocks to settle on the sand
beside their seagull kin

Esperance to Meridian Free Camp
Day 31 Sunday July 23

Hope for Owls

My spirits lift as we head west along the South Coast Highway. Being on the road is a happy place for me, the journey often more enjoyable than the destination, no matter how grand, or beautiful, or sublime.

The road's visible to the horizon and it's good to know of approaching roadtrains but there's little traffic. It's the off season and we're a long way from major centres and more popular attractions. We never have the radio on, or play music, and rarely talk, except to discuss break times and possible camp sites. There's so much else to do, such as look and think and simply be.

The roadside growth shifts subtly with the advent of early wattles amongst late banksias, and the darker greens of native cypress that sit like cool islands amid the mallees' bronze. Ravens rule the verges and the occasional hovering raptor rules the sky.

We are near Ravensthorpe when a dashboard warning light comes on as it did on our 2021 Outback journey. Again it's the fuel filter light. The manual tells us to immediately visit our local dealership, advice received with a certain amount of derision. Once out of the city, a dealership with the required part might be several hundred kilometres away, if you're lucky, and if you're not, you might be waiting weeks for the part to be shipped in.

Outback fuel can be dirty and as well as having the 4x4 serviced before we left, we invested in 24 hr, 7 days a week Roadside Assistance. On the 2021 journey, a mechanic drove 80 kms to change the filter but it's Sunday and the local representative's not answering his phone.

The people at Roadside Assistance are apologetic but we all know that nothing is going to happen before Monday and we head a few kilometres out of town to the Meridian Free Camp. A plaque tells me the meridian of 120 degrees east longitude runs through this spot, which serves as the baseline for Western Australian Standard Time. It explains the Free Camp's name and we pull up behind the first row of trees and set a fire.

Traffic sweeps past on the highway in front and there's a swathe of bulldozed trees behind, backed by heavily wooded hills. We're alone until the sky delivers its multitude of stars and then they're the type of company we welcome.

Owlless I

Sunshine warms my back
as I survey the dead
and broken trees
ghost-like
against the denser greens
of living trees behind

there's traffic noise
roadtrains, RV's, vans
and bird song that reveals itself
slowly
but not the birds

the sky darkens
and I hope for owls
but the night remains
empty of their calls

Owlless II

There are no owls tonight
and as the stars take charge
no birds at all
at least that I can hear
or see

but the trees know
what roosts amongst their branches
or brushes past their trunks
to disturb the litter
with its soft tread

and if they speak of it
it's not in words I know
or seek to know

my knowing of this world
already burden enough

Meridien Free Camp to Coalmine Beach
Day 32 Monday July 24

Blue-touched Wings

A quick visit to a mechanic at Ravensthorpe the next morning confirms our need to go to Albany (293 kms/182 mls further west) for a new fuel filter. Albany, a major regional city (population 40,000), is en route but we hadn't intended to stop there. We ring ahead and are in luck. They have the part and can fit it when we arrive.

Once there, we have to manoeuvre the van down a very tight service road and unhitch. A mechanic drives the 4x4 away and I'm a quarter of the way through my complimentary cup of tea when he brings it back, and we're on our way again carrying a spare filter.

The delay means it's later than we planned when we reach the hilly roads of tall timber country which are harder driving than the flat sparse country we've left behind. We've planned very few Free Camps on this trip and booked even fewer parks and I'm on a call to a park when the line cuts out, though not before I learn that recent rains make the entry road impassable.

A sign for a caravan park swings into view and on an impulse, we turn down it, and end up in one of the loveliest parks we've stayed at.

Coalmine Beach
Day 33 Tuesday July 25 to Day 36 Friday July 28

Fledgling

Calling Down the Rain

The kookaburra's calling down the rain
singing it in from somewhere else
and laughing as the air heavies up
with moisture

it seems as happy with the sky's dark grey
as I am with its blue-touched wings

drops pattern the path
announcing themselves
to my feet first
and then to my face
like the cool touch of
falling feathers

Tree-top Walk

I tell myself I will be like the birds
as I mount the steel-mesh steps
but I remain a human being
with vertigo

it's 40 metres at its zenith
but I force myself to look down
in hope of avian insights

birds have no fear of heights, I tell myself,
but no one knows the fledgling's thoughts
as it takes its first flight

to leave the nest is
a literal and metaphorical
leap of faith

and in the end we all must jump
or only know the confines
of the nest

Coloured Day

It's a coloured day of early sun
and later storms
and rainbow birds between

galahs the pink and grey of sunset clouds
a common bronzewing's penny shine
the show-off blue of fairywrens
the oystercatchers' scarlet beaks

a spotted scrubwren's fragile breast
as pale as early honey
and silver gulls all hunkered down
against a pallid wind

Water King

Galahs swirl
in noisy celebration of
the rain-drenched morning
as if they're responsible

while a kookaburra descends
in a long slow glide
of silent majesty

with no need
to fanfare its watery
deeds

Emus

There's a paddock full of
farm animals to the right
unremarkable
except they're emus

while in the paddock to the left
a single emu grazes

you get the sense it's escaped somehow
and thinks itself a hero
wild and free

but it's keeping company with sheep
while it's the other emus
who truly know their flock

Sailor

The sunset delivers no blaze of colour
but the blue-black clouds
break
to pour light on the water
and turn the waves to
silver

Venus appears
dressed in silver too

a pelican sets sail
on a solitary voyage
while somewhere up the beach

there are bongo drums

they keep an even rhythm
but evoke no wild yearning
and the pelicans on shore
remain earth bound

Skyway Waterway

Tall timbers line the highway
leaning in to leave
a strip of sky between
like a river

waterways give me back the sky
in reflections
brighter than the
real thing

but it's hard to judge
the real thing
when pelicans glide
on both

Morning Raven

This morning's raven
flies low through trees
black-glossed
with night time
rain

Ravens and Crows II

I've listened and watched
with strict attention
to experts describe
the difference between
ravens and crows

wanting to be correct
to not misidentify
to be reliable

but I can't snatch one from the skies
part its feathers
and check the colour of its down
and so I'm left with calls
which tell me nothing

Coalmine Beach to Meridian Free Camp
Day 37 Saturday July 29

Each Bird Call

Our decision to stay south on this journey means we've enjoyed mainly dry, sunny weather but the rain finally catches up with us. Cloudbursts make for wonderful sights along the coast and inland waterways but as the rain sets in and our site grows muddier, we decide to turn for home.

We've explored much of the surrounding area including the Valley of the Giants, between Walpole and Denmark, home to the immense Tingle Trees (that can grow for over 400 years and up to 75 metres/246 ft) and the Karri (that reaches over 90 metres/295 ft) but even without the Tingle and Karri trees, there's much to admire about the rain-drenched forests as we drive east.

It's 1,345 kms (835 mls) to the Western Australian border by the most direct route which still takes us 203 kms (126 mls) north to Norseman. A glance at any map of Australia shows how few roads there are in the Outback and fewer still that are sealed, and many of those are single-lane. Unsealed roads might be shut by local authorities after rain or be in good condition only after a grader's passed through, and it isn't always easy to discover when a grader's passed through. The blinding dust and windshield-smashing stones thrown up by roadtrains pose other hazards too.

Even so, we have travelled many unsealed roads and tracks on other journeys, mostly with no problems greater than dust, but on one memorable occasion, despite our low speed, we broke virtually everything possible inside the van. Having learned our lesson, we decide to repeat our westward route most of the way home, and that means our first stop is back at the Meridian Free Camp.

Music of Birds

We've been to this Free Camp before
but nothing's ever the same
and this time we're
not alone

a small campervan's holed up
behind some bushes
its single occupant's turned back
negating my urge to smile
and wave

as I pursue bird calls
in failed attempts
to match the songs
to owners

in the end I cease my chase
content to simply let their music
wash over
me

Meridian Free Camp to Salmon Gums
Day 38 Sunday July 30

Other Knowing

The benefit of retracing our steps is that we know where the easy access fuel stations are and we fill up at Ravensthorpe the next morning before we follow the South Coast Highway to Esperance, where it becomes the Coolgardie-Esperance Highway as we turn north to Salmon Gums. We don't bother to ring ahead this time and as we draw nearer, I wonder if it will be crowded, but there are even fewer campers there than our first visit and we pull into our previous site.

I'm better prepared this time to capture the mega-long ore train on my phone camera and get several videos which tell me it takes around 1 min 44 secs to pass. Again little is open in the small town but I find a packet of biscuits for afternoon tea and the park manager goes far beyond the call of duty to fill our empty gas bottle. The day is showery and the wet adds a glistening veneer to the salmon gums as I repeat my previous stroll around the town.

Drift of Feathers

The birds seem the same as
when we headed west
but now I know more of them
or perhaps more about myself

information doesn't occupy
separate spaces in our heads
but bleeds
into other knowing
to change it

and if we're lucky
and take the time to let it happen
wisdom can be made

not in big slabs
heavy with gravitas
but in small shining pieces
like the gloss on leaves
caught by the shifting sun

Salmon Gums to Baxter Free Camp
Day 39 Monday July 31

Nomads

This journey's been deliberately unhurried and we take advantage of the many stops along the way to break the drive. Sometimes we use the concrete picnic tables provided but most are graffitied and many strewn with rubbish despite the bins, and we set our camp chairs where things are cleaner. There's always ravens and magpies, and often honey-eaters and welcome swallows, to make the breaks enjoyable.

We pass the lakes, still as bright and reflective as mirrors, and stop in Norseman again for fuel and a supermarket visit. Every supermarket has its quirks and this one is dim in parts, but I know where things are hidden now and I'm in and out fast.

The Coolgardie-Esperance Highway changes its name again to the Eyre Highway as we head west through Balladonia to the Baxter Free Camp (or Rest Area as many are called). Baxter Free Camp has toilets and a dump point and extensive tracks and camping enclaves full of campers, I discover, as I wander off to stretch my legs. We are content to set our fire nearer the highway and later share it with a lone female traveller camped nearby who reveals her grief at being widowed.

There are many people on the road and most are generous in sharing their experience of the state of highways and tracks, Free Camps and parks, and in gifting personal stories. Some have endured terrible things and it's clear that, for some, the suffering is still raw, but their stories confirm my belief that journeying has a profound capacity to heal. The extraneous demands of life are shucked off, along with noise and business, to leave behind the core matters of eating and sleeping and thinking and simply being. Clock-measured time becomes irrelevant too, replaced by dawn and sunrise, sunset and dusk, the first bird call and the last.

Most people on the road are older and some are permanent travellers. Those who aren't commonly spend up to five months a year (usually between May and September) chasing the warmer weather of northern Australia. Retirement offers the opportunity to travel and I wonder whether, given the prevalence of nomadism in early human society, more younger people would be on the road too, were it financially possible. I also wonder whether we would be happier as nomads, where constant movement prevents us accumulating the material things that ultimately fail to make us happy.

Ravens Resplendent

There are rubbish bins at every stop
ex-oil drums painted yellow
and topped with metal mesh
hinged to put in rubbish
heavy to keep the ravens out

but ravens slide their heads
between the gaps
to extract their prizes
and make spaghetti with the mesh

the ground is streamer-strewn
in celebration of their avian skills
but it's rubbish still
despite its festive shape

Besieged

We set a fire
and are besieged by yellow-throated miners
on nearby branches
and on the arms of chairs
briefly vacated

accustomed to the scraps
of passing tourists
they hang around
acrobatic
and thick
as flies

Baxter Free Camp to 10 Peg Free Camp
Day 40 Tuesday August 1

No Bird Call

The days are bright and fine as we cross the border back into South Australia. There's no Quarantine Station until Ceduna, 480 kms (298 mls) further east. This always seems odd to me, given goods contaminated with pests and diseases could be discarded all along the way. We've already eaten, used up, or binned the prohibited things on the list, but it's the Quarantine Officer who has the final say and there's usually something allowed we've discarded, or something confiscated we thought allowed.

The 10 Peg Free Camp (as the name suggests) is about ten kms into South Australia and we pull in and set up. We had a coffee break here heading west and know its got that magic thing called Internet reception. My husband catches up on news and emails in the van while I set off to explore the maze of tracks. I'm keen to know whether they extend to the cliffs and give a view of the Great Australian Bight. There are many campers in the enclaves along the way but I turn back before I reach the end, besieged by flies and worried my appalling sense of direction will get me lost.

This journey's mainly been fly-free but in some parts of the Outback, flies can make being outside impossible even when wearing a fly net, and so it is here. I swat the flies away as I search for birds then give up and retreat to the van until dusk. The flies are still troublesome even in the evening's cool but I stand my ground. There's a supermoon tonight I want to see but our campsite's hemmed in by trees and the moon's not visible until it clears them. And then it's so glorious I even forget the flies.

Egg-shell Blue

There's a supermoon hanging huge
and silver
below the egg-shell blue of sky
in the pinkish part of dusk

the air has cooled but the flies
are reluctant to depart

there are no bird calls
no creak of branches
no rustle of leaves disturbed
just the hum and buzz
and stick of flies

10 Peg Free Camp to Whitewell Tank Free Camp
Day 41 Wednesday August 2

Ravens Eat

The next day dawns windy and the wind strengthens as the day goes on. We've never travelled with a tail wind (which I doubt exists, especially when cycling!) and head winds can more than double fuel costs. Today's wind is from the side which makes for a hard drive. We're pulling a big van with a big, heavy vehicle but each gust rocks us and roadtrains toss us about. It's less than 200 kms (124 mls) to our planned stop at Whitewell Tank and we're happy to pull in before noon. Unsurprisingly, we're the only campers there and take the prime position facing the gate.

We were here on Day 18 (July 9) on our eastward journey which seems like a lifetime ago. One of the benefits of journeying is how quickly old lives and cares are left behind. Fellow campers dribble in throughout the day until, by evening, the perimeter is full and vans are lining up across the middle.

We have an uninterrupted view of the moonrise this time and while technically no longer a supermoon, the moon is enormous, golden, and cloud-striped, and people are out and about with their cameras enjoying the sight.

Death Feeds Life

Ravens launch
hit the wind wall, stall
and think better of their direction
too smart to fight a foe
that keeps on blowing

they fly low and make
a meal of other creatures
that stayed too low
or stayed too slow
for traffic

ravens eat to fill their bellies
not for payback or historic debt
death feeds life
as it always has

No Medals

The day's given way to dusk
but the wind still blows
and stills the birds
except the wagtail
at dance amongst the grass

a pair of welcome swallows
sweeps on past
riding the wind's tail
it's different when they turn
and battle into it

there are no medals given here
for bravery

Whitewell Tank Free Camp to Penong
Day 42 Thursday August 3

Superb Fairywren

The sights are familiar as we journey on but no less spectacular. The Nullarbor Plain stretches away to our left in all its glorious pinks, rust-reds, and sage-greens and the intense blue sweep of the Southern Ocean forms the horizon to our right. This whole area is familiar not just because we passed this way a little over three weeks ago but because in 2021 we explored the nearby Fowler's Bay, known for its magnificent creamy sand dunes, whales, and reflective pools.

It's another short drive (about 150 kms/93 mls) to Penong and by then the day's turned showery. Being early, we have our choice of sites, and choose a drive-through, then have lunch before I revisit Penong's fascinating Windmill Museum and the town's corrugated iron buildings.

The park soon fills up and we chat to travellers who are mainly going west. This is consistent with this trip where most of the vans seem headed in the opposite direction. We try to keep outside popular traveller times, choose less popular routes, and avoid school holidays where anything deemed a tourist attraction becomes crowded. It means we can stay flexible by not needing to book ahead. It also means we've enjoyed deserted beaches, bush disturbed only by bird calls, and the deep silence of the Outback's dusk. The only real crowd on this trip has been the stars.

Dancers on the Road

A superb fairywren dances on the road
and as our vehicle straddles it
I hope it stilled
but when did a superb fairywren
ever still
except in death?

dead pigs litter the verges
or pieces of dead pigs
black bristled
torn apart by
B-doubles or roadtrains

feral animals are neither grieved
nor wanted
except by ravens

rich pickings

black on black
the handsome plumage
of the living
against the soiled skin
of the dead

Penong to Kimba Free Camp
Day 43 Friday August 4

Lazy Wingbeats

It's just over 300 kms (186 mls) to our next Free Camp at the Kimba Recreation Reserve but our first stop along the way is the Quarantine Station at Ceduna. The pleasant Quarantine Officer confiscates a couple of forgotten tomatoes and I learn I had no need to throw out the honey. There's nothing to be annoyed about though thanks to the sight of the sweep of sunny aqua water just over from the highway.

Ceduna is a gorgeous area we've explored at length on another journey but we still manage to miss the turn directly after the Quarantine Station and have to revisit some of the town to find our way back to the highway.

Lunch is in the small town of Poochera (population less than 100) which, like many other small towns along the railway line, is marked by towering grain silos. Poochera is traveller friendly with picnic tables, clean public toilets, and a basic caravan park for those who want to stay. I later learn the town has a major claim to fame in the shape of a prehistoric ant.

It's early on a sunny afternoon when we pull into the Recreation Reserve at Kimba, and there are lots more vans here than on our July 6 visit, one of which turns out to be our neighbour from Penong. Journeying in the Outback invariably means bumping into people you've chatted to or shared campfires with before. Travellers refuel at the same few roadhouses and use the same Free Camps or caravan parks when they travel the same route because that's all there is.

There's still plenty of room because most campers prefer to be near the ablution block. Our early afternoon arrival leaves lots of time for me to explore Kimba on foot which I've never done before. Like many older Outback towns, Kimba (established 1915) has many really interesting corrugated-iron buildings (often hidden behind more recent constructions) as well as its own terrific example of Silo Art (silos decorated with murals of iconic Australian scenes). And later, back at camp, I get to watch some truly wonderful starling murmurations.

Not Long Dead

Ravens are eating a galah
not long dead
its head propped up
as if about to fly
but it's the ravens that rise
in lazy wingbeats
to avoid our tyres

I wonder if bird eating bird is
cannibalism
or simply a really good feed

we excuse the raptors hunting
their fellow winged-creatures
but for some strange reason
the ravens' opportunism
seems less grand

Starlings Sweep

Starlings sweep the sky's perimeter
faster than my camera's focus
then slower
a mass dance that magics
from blurred to sharp
and back again

Kimba Free Camp to Port Augusta
Day 44 Saturday August 5

Against the Wind

It's a short 156 kms (96 mls) drive to Port Augusta, a journey made enjoyable thanks to the Gawler Ranges' blue sprawl and Lake Gilles Conservation Park's salt lakes but we haven't gone far before the police wave us off the road.

It's common in the Outback for large pieces of mining equipment to be moved by road and because they often occupy more than a lane, are preceded by escort vehicles with orange flashing lights. Really big pieces of equipment occupy the entire road and are preceded by police cars who clear the road of on-coming traffic. We wait on the verge and two trucks trundle into view carrying what looks like giant buckets. It's a short and interesting delay and then we are on our way again.

The highway descends from the Arcoona Plateau in a panoramic sweep I never tire of and then the sparkling waters of the Spencer Gulf come into view again. To the north, the gulf narrows to the Pirie-Torrens corridor, a depression that enjoys water flows only when Lake Torrens (a sink) overflows (twice in recorded history), while to the south the gulf sprawls between the Eyre and Yorke Peninsulas, which we've explored on other trips.

We stay at the same park in Port Augusta as previously, and arriving early gives me ample time to walk back to the Joy Baluch Bridgeand, as on my earlier visit, use its vantage point to watch the birds and enjoy the gulf's stunning vistas.

Less Prettily than Feathers

The gulls have painted the bridge-stones
white with waste they shed
less prettily than feathers
they launch at my approach
to hang eye-level
breasts a pristine white
unlike the stones
they quit

Port Augusta to Tailem Bend
Day 45 Sunday August 6

Aerofoiled like Wings

Our route back to Victoria is usually the more westerly one of Peterborough, Burra, Tailem Bend and then over the Victorian border to Kaniva but this time we head more southerly. We've got a few days to use up at the end of the trip (due to a booking for caravan maintenance in Melbourne) and we decide to spend them at Port Fairy, a lovely little town on Victoria's south western coast where we've holidayed for many years in hot and sunny January.

We set off down the Augusta Highway through the less familiar territory of Snowtown and Lochiel, skirt Port Pirie and hope to skirt Adelaide too but, thanks to a bit of Google confusion, we end up in peak hour traffic in lanes barely wider than the van. I'll admit that towing a caravan in traffic through an unfamiliar city is not my idea of fun, but we emerge unscathed into the picturesque Adelaide Hills, continue on through Murray Bridge, and reach Tailem Bend in early afternoon.

The park services a range of speedway events in the surrounding area and is enormous. We've stayed here before and as per our previous visits, there are no major events in progress and the park is half empty. The sites are roomy, but more importantly for my husband who's a keen AFL (Australian Football League) supporter, the park has Internet reception and he settles down for the afternoon to watch his team play.

I take a walk to the local minimart to stock up on junk food (necessary to watching any sporting event!) then spend the rest of the day wandering the park, chatting with fellow campers, and loitering in the large, treed area at the back in search of birds.

Less Forgiving than Feathers

I look for birds as we drive
but the air seems empty
only the thwack of wind turbines
breaks the silence

their broad blades are aerofoiled
like wings
but prove less forgiving
than feathers

Birdish Reason

Noisy miners are giving a raven a hard time
with no let up to their dive and dart
despite the raven's call of enough!

it's on the march out of there or on the wing
but maybe the fight is all pretence
a show put on for some birdish reason
unknown to me

Tailem Bend to Port Fairy
Day 46 Monday August 7

Settle Where They Will

The Dukes Highway takes us south, becoming the Western Highway when we cross into Victoria near Bordertown. We turn sharply south at Kaniva and follow the Kaniva-Edenhope Road to Edenhope (population 946) where we break for lunch. Our last larger town is Casterton (population 1658) before we pass through smaller settlements such as Merino (population 249).

These are neat little rural towns typical of Victoria but we've visited few of them before. We normally approach Port Fairy from Melbourne to the east, and when we quit Victoria, we do so from further north. The roads are sealed but single-lane, windy and bumpy, and the little traffic we encounter belongs to local farmers and tradesmen.

The countryside is lush and full of deep greens which, after the sprawling rusts and sage-greens of the Outback, seem as neat and manicured as a garden.

Sulphur-crested Cockatoos

Water lakes the paddocks
to reflect the cattle grazing
hoof-deep
and the sulphur-crested cockatoos
that rise
bright as snow
to settle again
like autumn leaves
of white

Port Fairy
Day 47 Tuesday August 8 to Day 49 Thursday August 10

Night's Deep Silence

Port Fairy is also wetter, greener, and cooler (as expected) than on our January breaks but the ocean has a special charm in winter. There are many quiet silvers, greys and whites, the beaches are unmarked by prints, and the sunsets and rises have more clouds to splash their colours. The cool means I can walk any time of day, not just early morning to avoid the heat, and I repeat all my usual walks as well as walk in the evening and night when the birds are less disturbed by others.

Solitary Wingbeats

The sunset gifts the lake
a pink so deep it stains the ducks
adrift on its still surface

other birds gather on a saltier shore
masked plovers
ravens
silver gulls
a single white-faced heron

there are squabbles
and soarings
and solitary wingbeats
until
all are swallowed
by the night's deep
silence

Soft Chocolate Browns

Birds land besides me
sparrows
their soft chocolate browns
light and dark
their bodies
nicely shaped

I know
humanity's contempt for the common
and as I watch them
(they're inclined to hang about)
I feel blessed they've gifted me
this glimpse of their
small beauty

Ducks of Gold and Teal

The wind robs the small lakes
of reflections
but there's still plenty to see
afloat

ducks of gold and teal
a moorhen's flashing beak
a flotilla doing its own thing
with the harmony
of a careless
murmuration

The Usual Crew

The beach is windswept
and the birds the usual crew
of silver gulls, plovers, ravens
plus the songs of birds
unseen

I ponder what device to use
to sort some names
and at my need to name them
as if to name grants power

it's not a new idea

the prayers of priests
the shaman's chant
the magic-maker's spells

intent on binding

perhaps the hardest task of all
is to let things be
and to know that it's
enough

Port Fairy to Melbourne
Day 50 Friday August 11

In the Company of Birds

There's an odd thing that happens whenever I near the end of a journey. As the familiar outskirts of Melbourne come into view I don't feel like I've been away. The sights and sounds and smells and sense of all I've experienced become as ephemeral as a dream that slips away on waking. Even landscapes as different as Norway and Scotland, where I spent several months in 2022, failed to hold their place in my mind as mundane tasks like washing travel clothes, restocking the pantry, and getting the garden under control took over.

And yet, no one returns from a journey unchanged. Every less familiar (or wholly unfamiliar) sight and sound and smell and sense alters us, sometimes subtly, sometimes dramatically. I remember with absolute clarity every aurora I saw in the Norwegian sky, the passing glories of its snow-capped mountains pinked by the rising sun, and the cloudbursts and sunbursts of the Scottish Highlands, and more recently, the sweeping dome of the Outback skies in all their wondrous iterations, the aqua seas with their white sands, and the tan, black, and silver-white of still or wind-whipped inland pools. And I know that every one of them has enlarged my spirit and soul.

I ended my book *Journey: Seeking the Sacred, Spirit and Soul in the Australian Wilderness* with an observation of two sulphur-crested cockatoos on my neighbour's fruit and nut trees, but the trees are gone (thanks to the block being scraped for redevelopment) and the birds along with them.

So, what of the birds I chose to write about on *this* journey? They have always been there but now my awareness of them is keener and their healing of me deeper. In a suburb full of traffic noise and human chatter, I hear the subtle layers of their songs, close and distant, see the flash of plumage pass overhead, or beside, or in bright mosaics amid the trees, and feel their comforting beauty in a world that is often ugly. I breathe more easily and am more easily delighted by all I see.

My birds came back to me and for that I am grateful.

Willie Wagtail

As the quiet gives way to city traffic
I think of the birds I've seen
or heard or sensed on *other* treks
in redder desert country

the wedge-tailed eagles
staring down the trucks
as they feast on roadkill
or at rest upon the thermals

in the endless blue

and the smaller hawks
cream-breasted
a hover
above some softer prey

and in Gulf Country
the jabiru and brolga
and snowy egret slender-legged
in still inland water
while above
the black and whistling kites
in constant motion

and I wonder which birds will become
mementos of *this* trek
through Australia's southern wilderness
of vast inland sweeps and
broken coasts
the black gloss of ravens and
the honey-eaters' flash

the gulls of pristine silver and
the oyster-catchers' crimson beaks
the ospreys braced against the wind
on some storm-lashed ledge

and the birds smaller, more mundane
that do little to announce themselves
in call or plumage or pure aesthetic clout
but stick in the memory
because of their unexpectedness
on beaches and deserted tracks
in Free Camps and curated parks
on walks where my gaze searches out
the exotic

only to be caught by
a flash of black and white
a rocking tail
as regular as a ship
in swell

a companion always just ahead
in zigzag across the path
the sexes the same
the insect hunt the same
the bird familiar
but made afresh
as the world is made afresh
by the company of birds

I hope you enjoyed *In the Company of Birds – Poems from an Outback Odyssey*. **Authors need reviews!** It is how our readers find us. I would love you to leave an honest review on Amazon, Goodreads, or another of your favourite reader sites. If the inner journey intrigued you, read on.

Works by K S Nikakis

Non Fiction

Journey: Seeking the Sacred, Spirit and Soul in the Australian Wilderness – For fans of Joseph Campbell's hero journey

When we set out into the wilderness, what is it we really seek?

Do we seek new sights or do we seek new selves? And are we really on one journey or on two?

Journeying fifteen thousand kilometres into Australia's blood-red heart, Nikakis discovers that every journey is perilous, for travellers risk carrying the clutter of their outer lives with them; a clutter that blinds them to the other journey they crave; that of the inner soul-journey into a deeper understanding of self.

To enter Australia's vast Outback wilderness, is to enter a place of endless horizons; a place doused with brilliant gold dawns and dazzling sunsets; a place silvered by star-encrusted night skies and, most importantly, a place of hidden sacred places in whose deep stillness our inner journeys can at last unfold.

In the spirit of travellers like Robert Macfarlane and Scott Stillman, Nikakis asks what it is we really see, feel and understand when we follow in the steps of those who have gone before us deep into the wilderness.

Drawing on her Ph.D. in Joseph Campbell's hero myth, and using original poetry and novel extracts, Nikakis takes us on this second journey; a journey of the sacred, spirit and soul, where our inner selves finally have the time and space to gift us richer and more fully-realised lives.

Fantasy Novel Series

Angel Caste 5 book series
Book 1 Angel Blood

Street-kid, thief, criminal: Viv is desperate to change her life.

On day release from jail to attend the funeral of her father, a violent drunk she feared and despised, her real father turns up, the powerful angel Archae Kald. He offers to reunite Viv with the mother she thought dead and, determined to find the only person who has ever loved her, Viv travels through a rift to the male angel world of Ezam.

Kald assigns his protégé, the beautiful angel Thris, to guide Viv to her mother. It is Thris's job to keep Viv safe in the Rynth, the vast tangle of worlds she never knew existed. But Viv is deeply damaged from her life on the streets and in no mood to trust anyone, even an angel with a face to die for. They set out, but as the complications multiply, disaster follows.

Thris might be eons old, but he knows little about females, especially ones who are half human. Like his closest friends, Ash and Ky, all he wants to do is transcend but when he and Viv stumble into the acrid world of Moth Fold, and Viv's latent angel traits emerge, transcendence seems the last thing possible.

After a devastating attack, Viv ends up lost and alone in the Rynth. Will she survive to continue the search for her mother? Or end her days in an alien world?

If you like your female heroes feisty, your male angels glorious, your fantasy worlds filled with brilliant landscapes and a dash of romance, you will love *Angel Blood*, Book 1 in the five book fantasy series *Angel Caste*.

Buy *Angel Blood* today to start your amazing adventure with Viv and Thris in the wild worlds of the Rynth.

Book 2 Angel Breath

Viv can survive on the streets, but can she survive in the Rynth?

Thris is gone, his exquisite body torn apart, and borne away by Ash and Ky. Viv fears she will never see him again, but there is no way she is turning back. She journeys on through the Rynth, narrowly escaping murderous landscapes and worlds full of savage creatures. Her life on the streets might have been a nightmare, but at least it taught her how to run, hide, and out-wit pursuers.

And then, when all seems lost, Thris returns. Viv is overjoyed, but her happiness is short-lived. He isn't the angel he was, and he isn't alone. Ky is with him, and Ky hates Viv. The feeling is mutual, but Ky's terror of the Rynth adds to their peril and they don't get far before they are besieged by savage, long-armed creatures. When Ky is injured, Thris is confronted with a terrible decision, and must abandon Viv to save him.

Viv journeys on but stumbles into a war zone. Desperate to escape, she is determined to take the next rift out, but finds a little girl, the sole survivor of a massacre. Recognizing the chance to make amends for the accident that landed her in jail, Viv delays the search for her mother, to take the little girl to safety.

But in an alien, war-torn world, it is all but impossible to tell friend from foe, and when the little girl falls ill, Viv must take a terrible risk. Will Viv manage to save the little girl? Or will the fighting cost them both their lives?

If you like your female heroes feisty, your male angels glorious, your fantasy worlds filled with brilliant landscapes and a dash of romance, you will love *Angel Breath*, Book 2 in the five book fantasy series *Angel Caste*.

Buy *Angel Breath* today to continue your amazing journey with Viv and Thris through the wild worlds of the Rynth.

Book 3 Angel Bone

Viv didn't abscond from jail to become someone else's prisoner, but that seems to be her fate.

As chance would have it, she resembles a people called the elddra, and that makes her both despised and desired. It also makes friends few and far between. Viv is desperate to deliver the little girl to safety, take a rift out, and resume the search for her mother, but dodging the new world's warring factions proves harder than she thinks.

As they journey on through strange and hostile lands, the little girl's trust and affection for Viv grows, and Viv is surprised by her own feelings of fierce protectiveness. And then, as they near safety, disaster strikes. They are overtaken by fighters and separated. Viv is seized and when the fighters are annihilated by a second force, their leader assumes she is one of the enemy. Prevented from executing her on the spot, the leader condemns her to a slower, more painful death.

In his own world, Thris struggles to care for Ky who is traumatized by his time in the Rynth, and when Ky flees, they end up imprisoned in a maze-like world where the only way out is a death-trap. Their hopes for rescue lie in Ash, but Ash is trapped too, entranced by a world of shining light, and unaware of his friends' plight.

Will Viv survive to be reunited with the child she loves? Or will she lose her too, as she has lost her mother and Thris?

If you like your female heroes feisty, your male angels glorious, your fantasy worlds filled with brilliant landscapes and a dash of romance, you will love *Angel Bone*, Book 3 in the five book fantasy series *Angel Caste.*

Buy *Angel Bone* today to continue your amazing journey with Viv and Thris through the wild worlds of the Rynth.

Book 4 Angel Bound

Viv thought things couldn't get any worse, but she is about to be proved wrong.

Disfigured by the ordeal she has somehow managed to survive, she realizes her grotesque appearance prevents her continuing her search for her mother and ends any hope of a future with Thris.

But Viv's angel blood is strong and, aided by its healing, she sets out to find the little girl. She is helped by a man whose kindness is something she has never experienced before, and love blossoms. He demands her trust, but haunted by images of witch-burnings, Viv daren't reveal what she really is. Complications multiply until being with him, and the child she loves, seems all but impossible.

Thris is bound by his pledge to guide Viv to her mother, and returns, but his search for Viv ends so catastrophically, that he yearns for death. All Viv's nightmares come true when she discovers his fate, but saving him, might cost the lives of countless others.

In Thris's absence, Ky and Ash uncover warnings about a trinity of angels the three of them resemble but who disappeared eons before in mysterious circumstances. The warnings about their fate are fragmentary, as if they have been deliberately destroyed.

Can Viv save the angel she loves? Or will she lose him and everything else she has come to care about?

If you like your female heroes feisty, your male angels glorious, your fantasy worlds filled with brilliant landscapes and a dash of romance, you will love *Angel Bound*, Book 4 in the five book fantasy series *Angel Caste*.

Buy *Angel Bound* today to continue your amazing journey with Viv and Thris through the wild worlds of the Rynth.

Book 5 Angel Blessed

It seems Lady Luck has smiled on Viv at last. Or has she?

When Viv is offered the chance of a home with the little girl she loves, she grabs it but then the child is snatched. To rescue her, not only must Viv battle the little girl's enemies, but those who love the child as well.

The perilous quest leaves Viv horribly injured, and she ends up in a world where she is offered the opportunity to finally heal herself. It means opening herself to terrible new risks but also the possibility of securing the little girl's safety, once and for all.

She returns to the child's world but is pursued by those who believe she holds the key to their deepest desires and, as their threats escalate to violence, Thris reappears. Viv's happiness soon turns to dread, as he reveals a threat that could destroy the little girl's world, as well as his own. Thris joins with Ky and Ash in a desperate fight to avoid the impending catastrophe and as events build to a climax, Viv prepares to sacrifice everything for those she loves.

Will Viv's search finally deliver her the loving home she craves? Or will she, and those she cares about, end their lives in the cataclysm that threatens?

If you like your female heroes feisty, your male angels glorious, and your fantasy worlds filled with brilliant landscapes and a dash of romance, you will love *Angel Blessed*, the final book in the five book fantasy series *Angel Caste*.

Buy *Angel Blessed* today to conclude your amazing journey with Viv and Thris through the wild worlds of the Rynth.

Angel Caste – Complete 5 Book Series

A troubled half-angel, a beautiful angel guide, a binding promise . . .

Viv is on day release from jail to attend the funeral of the thug she thinks is her father, when she comes face to face with her real father, the powerful angel Archae Kald. If finding out she's a half-angel isn't shocking enough, Viv discovers her mother isn't dead after all but lost somewhere in the tangle of worlds called the Rynth.

Determined to find the only person who has ever truly loved her, Viv goes to Kald's angel world where he appoints the beautiful Thris as her guide. Thris is kind and caring, unlike the males Viv has known before, but after living on the streets, Viv finds it almost impossible to trust.

Friendship grows as Thris trains her to travel the rifts, but the Rynth is a dark and dangerous place, even for angels and, as Thris grows increasingly tempted by Viv's emerging angel traits, disaster strikes.

Viv journeys on alone and stumbles into a war zone where she finds a lost child. She pledges to take the child to safety but, as the war rages on, deciding who is friend and who is enemy becomes a deadly game of chance.

Bound by his promise to guide Viv to her mother, Thris embarks on a desperate search for her, but a greater threat confronts them both and, in the end, they must fight not just for their own lives, but for the lives of those they love.

The Kira Chronicles - 6 book series
Book 1 The Whisper of Leaves

A gold-eyed Healer, a prophecy, two brothers at war.

In seasons long past, twin gold-eyed princes sundered a kingdom. Rejecting his brother's warrior ways, Kasheron led his people away to establish the Tremen community of Allogrenia, deep in the great southern forests. Forgotten by the outside world and protected by the trackless trees, the Tremen flourish for seasons uncounted, upholding Kasheron's legacy of peace and healing.

All Tremen delight in the healing arts, but Kira is the greatest Healer of them all.

To the north of Allogrenia, drought grips the land, and the Shargh suffer. A herding people, they lost their grazing tracts to the Northern invaders years before, through long and bloody wars. As the drought tightens its grip, and their herd animals die, the chief's younger brother seizes on an ancient prophecy to snatch the chiefship for himself.

The prophecy links the Shargh's doom to a gold-eyed Healer, and Kira has gold eyes.

The Shargh attack with devastating consequences, and Kira must fight to save the wounded. But the Shargh wounds rot, no matter her skill, and as the blood-shed continues, Kira faces losing everything and everyone she loves.

Can Kira cure the Shargh wounds? Or will the Tremen community be destroyed? If you love your female heroes feisty, your fantasy worlds with sun-dappled forests, quiet owl-filled nights, and just the right dash of romance, you will love *The Whisper of Leaves*, Book 1 of the six book *The Kira Chronicles* series.

Buy *The Whisper of Leaves* today to enter the forest world of the Tremen and start your amazing adventure with Kira as she fights to save her people.

Book 2 The Silence of Stone

How can fire quench fire?

The Tremen are dying and Kira is in a deadly race against time to save them. Somewhere deep in the Warens' labyrinth of underground tunnels, lies the answer to a riddle and the cure to Shargh wounds.

To find it, she must defeat the tunnels' unmapped darkness *and* Kest, the blue-eyed, blond-haired Commander of the Protectors. As leader of the force Kasheron established to keep the Tremen safe, Kest is sworn to protect, and everything Kira does puts her at terrible risk.

As she fights to heal, and he to protect, they join in an uneasy alliance to save the people they love.

When Kira is made Tremen Leader, the stakes rise even further. The Tremen are riven by division and Kira must fight to stop the Tremen community from breaking apart. Desperate to find the cause of the Shargh attacks and stop the Tremen's suffering, she goes ever deeper into the Warens' perilous darkness. Kest searches too, his quest in the sunlit forests above.

When he and his men make a gruesome discovery, he realizes what drives the Sharghs' murderous attacks, but then he makes a deadly mistake.

As Kira learns more of her brutal lineage, she is confronted with the horrifying truth that to save her people, she must lose them forever. Can Kira preserve Kasheron's legacy of peace and healing? Or will all he fought for be swept away by the violence he fled?

If you love your female heroes feisty, your fantasy worlds with sun-dappled forests, quiet owl-filled nights, and just the right dash of romance, you will love *The Silence of Stone*, Book 2 of the six book *The Kira Chronicles* series.

Buy *The Silence of Stone* today to enter the forest world of the Tremen and start your amazing adventure with Kira as she fights to save her people.

Book 3 The Secrets of Stars

What truths lie hidden in the stars?

Kira is alone, her food all but exhausted, the forest and those she loves, far behind her. When she stumbles on a stranger under attack, she faces a terrible choice: betray everything Kasheron fought for or walk away.

The stranger, Caledon, knows a path over the mountains and has friends nearby who can help them, but Kira's quest is clear: go straight north, gain aid for her people, and return home.

They continue together but the Azurcades are perilous and when a terrible storm threatens to sweep them to their deaths, their journey becomes a battle for survival.

Kira's trust in Caledon grows and his gentleness rouses other, deeper feelings, but Caledon is ruled by forces that pose a lethal threat to her quest. She plans her escape, but new lands bring new enemies and she is taken prisoner.

Fleeing her captors, Kira finds herself with a people under Shargh attack. As the carnage mounts and she joins with their Healers to save the wounded, her stocks of fireweed run dangerously low. Caledon strives to regain her trust and the stakes escalate when he reveals terrible truths that threaten the Tremen's very existence.

As the slaughter continues and Kira embarks on a hazardous search for fireweed, disaster strikes and she is snatched by the Shargh warrior who has long hunted her. Can Kira survive to reach the north and finally deliver aid to her people? Or will her quest end at the Shargh's brutal hands?

If you love your female heroes feisty, your fantasy worlds with sun-dappled forests, quiet owl-filled nights, and just the right dash of romance, you will love *The Secrets of Stars*, Book 3 of the six book *The Kira Chronicles* series.

Buy *The Secrets of Stars* today to enter the forest world of the Tremen and continue your amazing adventure with Kira as she fights to save her people.

Book 4 The Thunder of Hoofs

Who is friend and who is enemy?

When Kira's Shargh captors are attacked, she finds herself a prisoner of those who might prove even deadlier. But then, in a heart-rending twist of fate, their leader is revealed to be the bearer of everything Kira most loved in the world *and* everything Kasheron most despised.

Kira hides her identity but her subterfuge is discovered and the dangers multiply. Her quest is to gain aid from her northern kin, but the forests that hid the Tremen from enemies, also hid them from friends, and there is no help for a people without alliance or treaty. To make matters worse, the northern histories tell a very different story of the great Healer Kasheron.

To aid the Tremen, Kira must turn south again, to where Caledon will bring the Tremen fighters but she and the northern leader share a powerful attraction and he's determined to keep her safely in the north, far from the Shargh.

Desperate to learn of Kira's fate, Caledon journeys north too and they are reunited, but his arrival generates antagonisms that threaten alliances and treaties alike. As Caledon strives to decipher the stars' intent, the stakes escalate, and he fears following his heart could cause the deaths of countless others.

Kira is no slave to the stars and, driven by her duties as leader, sets out for the south. Besieged by squalling winds and icy storms, her escort comes under Shargh attack and

she finds herself in a desperate flight through the night in a terrifying attempt to outrun them. But Shargh hunters lie in wait, and in a deadly rain of spears, her mare goes down.
Can Kira survive to finally deliver aid to her people? Or will her quest end in the wind-swept darkness?

If you love your female heroes feisty, your fantasy worlds with sun-dappled forests, quiet owl-filled nights, and just the right dash of romance, you will love *The Thunder of Hoofs*, Book 4 of the six book *The Kira Chronicles* series.

Buy *The Thunder of Hoofs* today to enter the forest world of the Tremen and continue your amazing adventure with Kira as she fights to save her people.

Book 5 The Crying of Birds

Must Tremen healing bow before Terak swords?

Kira's deepest fears are realized when the Tremen are forced from the forests to join the devastating conflict on the plain. To add to her guilt, she can't remain with the people she leads but must go north. Sarnia has no healing, and if the fighting spreads, their wounded will die.

Leaving behind those she loves, she endures the perilous journey back to Sarnia, only to confront powerful forces determined to keep the ways of the despised Healer Kasheron out of the city. As Kira fights to create a place of healing, aid comes from an unexpected quarter, but a healing place without fireweed will save no lives.

Kira's search for fireweed grows increasingly desperate and then her worst nightmare comes true when the person she loves most in the world is mortally wounded. As the fighting drags on and winter deepens, the injured flood in and Kira's struggle to save them takes a deadly toll.

In the south, the Shargh tribes join, and Tierken makes a terrible mistake that puts Sarnia at risk. Distrust weakens their forces and as the bloodshed grows, treachery promises to deliver a Shargh victory. And then, as Tierken and his men fight for their very existence, word reaches him that Kira's life hangs in the balance. Faced with a terrible dilemma, he makes a choice that risks the destruction of his leadership in the north

Kira flees to the healing settlement of Kessom but to reach its sanctuary, she must navigate the raging torrent that claimed

Tierken's father. Will Kira survive to reach the healing she so desperately needs? Or will her journey end in the watery darkness?

If you love your female heroes feisty, your fantasy worlds with sun-dappled forests, quiet owl-filled nights, and just the right dash of romance, you will love *The Crying of Birds*, Book 5 of the six book *The Kira Chronicles* series.

Buy *The Crying of Birds* today to enter the forest world of the Tremen and continue your amazing adventure with Kira as she fights to save her people.

Book 6 The Music of Home

What is the price of peace?

With the fighting over, Tierken pursues Kira to Kessom where she is overjoyed to be reunited with him, but neither have escaped the battles unscathed. Kira's health is fragile and Tierken's aggression is honed from months of fighting. To add to the complications, Tierken's enemies in Sarnia have taken full advantage of his absence in the south.

Angered by their scheming and frustrated by Kira's refusal to bend to his will, his arguments with her escalate until Kira realizes the breach between the Tremen and Terak is too large for her to mend. Her hopes for a future with Tierken shattered, she sets out for home, but the Sarsalin is full of dangers and enemies lie in wait.

Caledon waits too as he struggles to reconcile his own want of Kira with the wants and needs of the stars. They travel south together and when they come upon a sick Shargh child, Kira begins to understand the brutal consequences of the fighting, and that bloodshed can only ever seed more bloodshed.

Desperate to prevent future warfare, Kira resolves to offer the Shargh people healing, despite knowing it will likely cost her life. But when she reaches the Shargh settlement, she makes a shocking discovery that changes everything.

There are Shargh women there who crave peace as she does, but she comes face to face with the man who believes her death will deliver him everything he desires, and as the final chilling part of the last Telling unfolds, she realizes for the first time, what is truly precious to her and what is worth fighting for.

Will Kira survive to return to all she loves, or make the ultimate sacrifice as she strives for peace?

If you love your female heroes feisty, your fantasy worlds with sun-dappled forests, quiet owl-filled nights, and just the right dash of romance, you will love *The Music of Home*, the final installment in *The Kira Chronicles* series.

Buy *The Music of Home* today to enter the forest world of the Tremen and complete your amazing adventure with Kira as she fights to save her people.

The Kira Chronicles – Complete 6 Book Series

A gold-eyed Healer, a prophecy, two brothers at war.

In seasons long past, twin gold-eyed princes sundered a kingdom. Rejecting his brother Terak's warrior ways, Kasheron led his people deep into the great southern forests and established the healing settlement of Allogrenia. The Tremen flourished, upholding Kasheron's legacy of peace and healing, and protected by the vast, trackless trees.

All Tremen delight in the healing arts, but Kira is the greatest Healer of them all.

To the north of Allogrenia, drought ravages the Shargh's land, and as their suffering escalates, the chief's younger brother seizes on an ancient prophecy to snatch the chiefship for himself. The prophecy links the Shargh's doom to a gold-eyed Healer, and Kira has gold eyes.

The Shargh attack with devastating consequences and Kira must fight to save the wounded, but the Shargh wounds rot, no matter her skill, and Kira finds herself in a deadly race against time. As the slaughter continues, she makes the horrifying discovery that the Shargh hunt *her*. To halt the attacks and save her people, she sets off for the North to seek aid from her long sundered warrior kin.

But the dangers beyond the forests exceed even the Shargh attacks. The Tremen detest their warrior kin but Terak's descendants have inflicted a worse fate on the Tremen. Kira's new-found love is torn apart by ancient hostilities and when trust turns to betrayal, it risks everything she has fought for.

As the battles rage on, Kira becomes increasingly sickened by the bloodshed. Desperate to end the suffering once and for all, she sets out on a quest that could cost her everything and everyone she loves.

Fantasy Novels

The Emerald Serpent

Check out the fabulous book trailer https://www.
youtube.com/watch?v=bGpKxnpCEMg

Betrayal, torture, death: Etaine lives on only to destroy those
who robbed her of everything she loved.

Seven years before, Etaine met fellow Ranger Cormac,
the he-Eadar she believed was her longed-for true-mate.
Emerald-eyed, white-skinned, and black-haired, the Eadar
had formed into Ranger bands to fight the Fada, invading
religious zealots determined to replace the Eadar's Serpent
Goddess with their own gods of stone.

The pure blood of the ancient Eadar runs strong in Etaine and
Cormac's veins, and their joining had the potential to open
the Emerald and Serpent Ways to them, old worlds only true
Eadar can enter. But their love affair goes tragically amiss,
with catastrophic consequences.

Etaine flees and as the years pass, slowly rebuilds her life,
but the Fada's attacks grow more ferocious, and the Eadar
are forced to fight for their very existence. When the Fada
mass to commit yet more bloody slaughter, and the bands
join in a final, desperate effort to defeat them, Etaine comes
under Cormac's command, the very last Eadar she ever
wants to see again.

Together they have a weapon that can destroy the Fada, but
to use it, Etaine must learn to trust again and Cormac to
Remember. And time runs short: the Serpent rises.

Don't miss the enthralling story of Etaine and Cormac's fight to defeat the Fada and revive the old worlds of the Eadar. Set in the ancient Caledonian Forest of Northern Scotland, with its misty crags and bright, rushing streams, *The Emerald Serpent* will delight those who love their fantasy with a touch of Celtic and a dash of romance.

Buy *The Emerald Serpent* today to share Etaine and Cormac's amazing quest to rid their beautiful worlds of the Fada threat.

Heart Hunter

Fleet is a young Sceadu hunter: skilled, strong, and fast. She hunts deep into the icy mountains, seeking meat for her people, for the rains have failed and plunged the Sceaudu into hunger.

Her hunts are hard, but she has much to look forward to. Soon she will be gifted her air-name by the Sceadu's shaman, and then she will be a full adult, and free to marry the man she loves.

But while Fleet is on hunt, the old shaman dies, and the new shaman visions a very different future for her: cross the frozen, ice-locked mountains and complete a perilous quest or lose the man she loves forever.

In a moment of anger and frustration, Fleet commits a terrible wrong and sets out into the frigid mountains to atone with her life. In a journey that takes her deep into the earth's darkest places, into strange new worlds, and even into Death itself, she discovers that only she can save her people. To survive, she must draw on every shred of her hunter strength, and doing the impossible, it turns out, is just the beginning.

If you love strong, independent female hunters, bright snowy landscapes, worlds where truth might lie in the mystical realms of a vision-quest, and a dash of romance, you will love *Heart Hunter*.

Buy *Heart Hunter* today to share Fleet's danger, joy, and discoveries in her quest to save her people and the man she loves.

The Third Moon

Where does the past end and the future begin?

Haunted by inherited memories of his people's dispossession and theft of their children, Warrain is just twelve years old when the nightmare repeats. But Warrain isn't living on Earth in the 21st Century, he is living on the planet Imago in the far flung future.

Five years before, Station One's Mech's got high on the opioid arrash, and in the bloodshed that followed, Warrain's scientific community were expelled from the Station, his father murdered, and his mother and unborn sibling lost to him.

The scientists carve out a rudimentary Station high in Imago's ranges, and Warrain's friends get on with their lives. Not Warrain; he climbs the Tors to stare down at Station One, dream of his mother and sibling, and plot revenge.

And then one day, everything changes. A third moon appears in the sky, one of Imago's life-forms calls him by name, and disease breaks out at Station One.

When the Mechs visit to seek help for their ill, Warrain seizes the opportunity to deal them a blow they will never forget. But the third moon brings changes that threaten them all and, to aid the life-form whose kind is being dispossessed and slaughtered, he must turn his back on the hate that has long sustained him and find another way to live.

If you are fascinated by the power of memory, the excitement of life on other planets, and like your fantasy with a dash of romance, you will love *The Third Moon*.

Buy *The Third Moon* today to share Warrain's life on Imago as he struggles to protect Imago's creatures and make the planet truly his home.

Messenger

In a world made deaf by hatred, who will hear the messenger?

Severine's world ends the day her family is murdered. Being raised in the loving community of gay Travelers always marked her as an outsider, but being female puts her in mortal danger. Women are scarce, precious, and hunted.

When chance brings Severine face to face with the father she has never known, he assigns the son of his murdered best friend to guard her. They soon clash. Severine believes all men are violent brutes and Jeph resents his freedoms being curtailed.

An uneasy understanding grows but Jeph is glad to deliver her to the Enclaves, a sanctuary her father has carved out in the mountains for his women and children. But there is no safety in a world broken by war and sickness and when violence follows her, Severine flees to the northern city of Andhaka in search of a home amongst her mother's people. Jeph follows, bound by loyalty to her father, but the north holds terrible dangers for him.

It's been years since Andhaka has welcomed outsiders with anything but bullets, and to survive and to protect Jeph, Severine must learn to use her enemies' weapons against them. As the stakes rise, she comes to understand the horror of her mother's loss, and what drove her father north seventeen years before. His quest becomes her quest, but she hasn't counted on the savage legacy that war and sickness have left behind, or on falling in love.

Can Severine succeed where her father failed? Or will her fate prove even deadlier than his? If you love your fantasy set in brilliant new worlds, with characters you really care about, and just the right dash of romance, you will love *Messenger*.

Buy *Messenger* today to share Severine's journey as she fights for a home, the man she loves, and a better world.

I Heard the Wolf Call My Name
Finalist Best YA Novel – 2019 Aurealis Awards

Jax is on the run from his past. A shifter from the island of Rua, he is trapped on the mainland amongst the despised Off-islanders. Even worse, he is in the military, with a less than exemplary military record.

So when he is ordered to pack up his kit and is flown away in the middle of the night, he is in no position to argue. And it isn't as if he has any other place to go.

Ten years before, when Jax was just twelve years old and in bird-form high above his island home, it blew to smithereens, leaving him the only survivor, or so he believes.

The mystery flight dumps him at a new base where he comes face to face with Matiu, the boyhood friend Jax thought was as dead as his previous life. The military want Jax for an important mission and Matiu wants Jax too, but for different reasons, but there is no way Jax is going to resurrect what took him ten long years to bury.

As the pressure on him ramps up, Jax flees but is confronted by something more deadly than his nightmarish memories. To stop the other Islanders suffering the same fate as his people, Jax must finally face who and what he really is and decide where he truly belongs.

Like stories that question what it means to be human? That escape the narrow definitions of friendship and love? If so, you will enjoy Jax and Anahera's journeys.

Buy *I Heard the Wolf Call My Name* to see the world through very different eyes.

The Dragon of the Drowned World (Young Adult)

When the earth shivers and shakes and the oceans rise over the lands, thirteen year old Jojo washes up on a strange shore. The adult survivors build a ramshackle settlement from the debris the ocean delivers, and make sense of their predicament by comparing themselves to Noah and his Ark.

But not everyone agrees and all Jojo wants is his family back.

He scours the beach each day looking for things that aren't broken or dirty and stumbles on a strange, silvery plate. When the plate is smashed by an older boy, Jojo stores the pieces in his secret cave, but then odd things start to happen. The ferocious blood crabs give way to him on the beach and when he's attacked by a giant serpent, it suddenly lets him go.

His fellow wash up, Lee, finds a strange, poisoned little creature and friendship grows as they team up to save it. Lee insists the creature is a griffin and Jojo's plate pieces belong to a loong or dragon but Jojo has enough problems without adding mythic creatures to the list.

When Lee's little creature takes to the skies and the adults set out to hunt it down, Jojo and Lee embark on a desperate quest to save it. But as their journey takes them ever deeper into danger and the plates seem to grow in power, Jojo fears the dragon might turn out to be the deadliest creature of them all.

Like adventure stories where mythic animals come alive? Where characters tackle the really big questions about life? You'll love *The Dragon of the Drowned World*.

Fantasy Short Stories

Take a peek at excerpts from my short stories.

The Gift – A Deep Fantasy Short Story #1

Thariel sat for a long time, surveying all around her, as if she ate the world that would soon be memory. Then she took the harness from the mare, and with soft words, thanked her and bade her farewell. Her own feet she turned towards the forest, tossing her face-plate aside as she went, so that her hair fell loose to her waist, then she discarded her chest-armour, the sword and dagger, her bow and quiver.

The trees closed in and she came at last to the lake Men call Menios and stood for a while on its shore. An owl cried and a mouse shrieked, and all around her the souls of the newly dead jostled in their journey to the void. She stepped into the water and the new life inside her quivered.

'Fear not, little one,' she whispered, in her own tongue. 'We are going home.'

The Tale of Prince Anura – A Deep Fantasy Short Story #2

I should have been happy, for she was beautiful. Dark rivers of curls, skin as white as moonlight on water, breasts softer than spawn, and she loved me well. But her chamber was small, no matter the comfort of her bed, and the old feelings of entrapment rose, as persistent as gas that bubbles from rot below still waters.

I sat at the casement and listened, as I had once loitered near the watery skin of the second world and waited. The moon grew large and small many times, but it came at last, as I knew it would. The soft lament on the night-time air, the song of a soul as confined as mine. It took me a journey of many days through the depths of a massive forest to find her tower.

Stone it was and sheer, and as remote as the third world's glimmer had once been. I sang to her and she answered with sweet melodies of her own and we made love as frogs do, with our voices. And when trust had built, she let down her shining ladder of golden hair.

Glass-Heart – A Deep Fantasy Short Story #3 *Finalist*
Best YA Short Story – 2019 Aurealis Awards

Geth moved amongst his band, exchanging quiet words while they waited. Some he had fought with since the Tallon's foul ships had first found their shores while others had come later, when the burn of cot and kin had sent them from their valleys.

Hate drove them but hate was no shield against arrow and knife. It was fighting skills that kept them hale, and Geth ensured they had them aplenty. He needed them living, not just for their own sakes and his, but for what would come later. When the Tallon's stain had been scoured away, the destroyed must be rebuilt.

Kyth sat alone and he went to her and gazed about. 'The glass-heart's fled, has it?'

'I sent her to a place of safety. She will come to me when it is over.'

'Safety was what I wanted for you!'

'And what I wanted for Nyar.' Her eyes caught the star-sheen as she looked up at him.

'But you can't always have what you want, can you, Ceannasai?'

Dragon Sprite – A Deep Fantasy Short Story #4

Genn rocketed straight upwards, not just because she enjoyed seeing the limitless blue sky before her, but because a Waiwin's wing shape made vertical flight harder for them. Orin didn't try to catch her but swept in circles around her, gaining height in an ever-narrowing spiral. It was a clever tactic and one Genn didn't believe he had thought of in the instant she had cleared the trees. He had obviously studied her strategies and developed a plan to counter them *or so he thought.*

Genn waited until the spiral narrowed to *axeel*, the minimum distance a Waiwin must keep from a Velven unless she *accepted* him, then swerved towards him, narrowing the distance between them. Orin's eyes flashed to black, shocked she *had* accepted him, but before he could act, she folded her wings and dropped.

The strength that had driven Orin's pursuit had surged to his wing-tendrils in anticipation of locking them with hers and he would struggle even to stay airborne until it flowed back.

Ghost Stream – A Deep Fantasy Short Story #5

It rained that day, a mighty deluge and as I watched the water sweep across the ground I wished I had made the water angry earlier. The rain did not last and the next morning the ground was dry as dust but that night I was woken by a roar. Worse still, was the pound of hoofs that told me the cattle ran in panic. The night was thick as I headed out with the stockmen, Billy by my side, to discover the river I had never seen flow, stormed along in full flood. I rode with the men to save the cattle but the water cut between us so that only Billy was with me as we drove the cattle back.

And then the water divided us too. I heard Billy's shout as I spurred after some breakaways, and then my horse was gone, and I was in the torrent, and the night turned in upon itself.

And now I linger here, dead but not at peace, when all I want is rest.

The White Stag – A Deep Fantasy Short Story #6

Tom wiped his shaking hand across his mouth and felt the temperature drop. Colder air settled in the holloway but this was something different and he sensed the start of another mind-tricking episode.

There was certainly nothing natural about the mist that swirled about him or the visitors it brought. At first Tom thought the figure he saw was a poacher with an ill-gotten pheasant slung about his shoulders but then he realised it was the hindmost walker in a line of other walkers. They were skin-clad, their naked backs and legs pale in the silvery light. The men carried small packs and spears, the women hide-wrapped bundles or small children. They went without speaking and then they were gone.

Rite – A Deep Fantasy Short Story #7

My memories have got pretty jumbled over the years. Sometimes I think I might've been a stockman who drowned when I chased cattle into a flooded river, refusing to let a mob of dumb-arsed beasts outsmart me, or maybe I was a tradie who wouldn't let a bit of water over the road get in the way of the quickest route home. Maybe I dived into a river I thought was deep, or likely didn't think at all beyond beating my mates in, or maybe I did none of these things. Yet in some weird way, I know I died in water, and that if there *is* more than one of me, we all went into the water and bloody well never came out.

I mightn't know how I ended up here, dead but somehow not dead, and a hell of a long way from anywhere I'd ever been before but I do know exactly where *here* is, thanks to the sign driven into the rock-hard ground. Its metal might be a bit rusty but what it says is still pretty clear to anyone who bothers to read it. The thing that's caught me, like a cat catches a mouse, is called a Quartz Blow, but I call it *the She*. The sign has a whole lot of guff about the chemical reactions that happen when volcanoes decide to fizz and how Quartz Blows are formed, but says nothing about how the She keeps me close.

www.ingramcontent.com/pod-product-compliance
Lightning Source LLC
Chambersburg PA
CBHW072006090426
42740CB00011B/2110